Rattlesnakes

Julie Fiedler

PowerKiDS press
New York

Published in 2008 by The Rosen Publishing Group, Inc.
29 East 21st Street, New York, NY 10010

First Edition

Editor: Jennifer Way
Book Design: Julio Gil
Layout Design: Kate Laczynski
Photo Researcher: Nicole Pristash

Photo Credits: Cover, p. 1 © www.istockphoto.com/Steve McSweeny; pp. 5, 11, 13, 17 © Shutterstock.com; p. 7 © www.istockphoto.com/Ronnie Wilson; pp. 9, 15 © SuperStock,Inc.; p. 19 © www.istockphoto.com/John Billingslea Jr.; p. 21 © www.istockphoto.com/David Rose.

Library of Congress Cataloging-in-Publication Data

Fiedler, Julie.
  Rattlesnakes / Julie Fiedler. — 1st ed.
      p. cm. — (Scary snakes)
  Includes index.
  ISBN-13: 978-1-4042-3834-3 (library binding)
  ISBN-10: 1-4042-3834-4 (library binding)
  1. Rattlesnakes—Juvenile literature. I. Title.
  QL666.O69F537 2008
  597.96'38—dc22
                                        2007004288

Manufactured in the United States of America

Contents

What Are Rattlesnakes?

Rattlesnakes are named for the rattles at the end of their tail that make noise. These snakes rattle their tail when they feel they are in danger. Rattlesnakes belong to a family, or group, of snakes called Viperidae. This family includes vipers and pit vipers.

Rattlesnakes are pit vipers. They have pits on their face that sense heat and help them know when **predators** or **prey** are near. Rattlesnakes live in North America in places like the desert, mountains, and even in water. Rattlesnakes are **venomous** and can kill people.

This is a western diamondback rattlesnake. Snakes use their tongue to help sense the world around them. It can tell a snake what kinds of animals are nearby.

The Rattle

Rattles are special scales made of a **protein** called keratin. That is the same protein that makes your fingernails. When rattlesnakes grow, they shed their skin. Part of the shed skin adds on to the tail to make the rattle. Rattles are very **fragile**.

The rattling sound is made when pieces of the rattle knock together. They can rattle as fast as 60 times per second! Rattlesnakes do not always make noise. The Santa Catalina Island rattlesnake is the only member of the rattlesnake family that does not have a rattle.

You can see that a bit of the tip of this rattlesnake's rattle has broken.

Fangs and Venom

Rattlesnakes have poisonous **saliva**, called venom. The venom of some rattlesnakes is so powerful that it can kill people.

When rattlesnakes bite, the venom goes into their prey through two long, hollow teeth, called **fangs**. Rattlesnakes can fold their fangs into their mouth when they do not need them. Fangs are fragile, but if they break off, rattlesnakes can grow new ones. Every 60 days, new fangs replace the old ones by locking into place where the old fangs were. When new fangs are moving into place, you can see rattlesnakes with two sets of fangs.

This rattlesnake's fangs are folded down into the biting position.

How Rattlesnakes Hunt

Rattlesnakes' heat-sensitive pits help them sense their prey when they are hunting. This is important for when they are hunting at night.

Venom helps rattlesnakes capture their prey. The venom stuns or kills the prey. Venom also helps rattlesnakes digest, or break down, their prey. Rattlesnakes eat mice, shrews, frogs, bird eggs, and lizards.

Rattlesnakes are eaten by many different animals. Their predators include large birds, such as hawks and herons.

Pit

This is a timber rattlesnake. Rattlesnakes don't always inject venom when they bite. A bite without venom is called a dry bite. All snake bites should be looked at by a doctor, though.

Rattlesnake Defenses

Rattlesnakes have **defenses**, such as **camouflage**, warnings, and striking. Camouflage is when an animal can mix in with its **habitat** in order to hide.

Rattlesnakes often make a rattling noise as a warning for their enemies to think twice about sticking around. If that does not work, rattlesnakes will strike, or bite. However, if they are surprised, they will sometimes strike without warning first.

Rattlesnakes strike quickly and can leap up to half of their body length when they bite. The best striking position is called a **coil**.

This rattlesnake is in its coil position. Rattlesnakes often move into a coil position before they strike. However, they can strike from any position!

Young Rattlesnakes

Female rattlesnakes give birth to live young, instead of laying eggs. This means that their young grow inside of them. Female rattlesnakes give birth to about 10 babies at a time. Rattlesnakes reach adulthood in about 3 years and many can live to be 20 years old.

Most rattlesnake babies leave their mother when they are one or two weeks old, after they have shed their first skin and have their first rattle. Young rattlesnakes sometimes see their mother again when they **hibernate**. They follow the mother's scent to her den.

Here you can see a group of adult female timber rattlesnakes and their young.

Sidewinders

Sidewinders live in desert areas in the United States and Mexico. They are tan with gray and brown markings to camouflage them in sand. They are 17 to 34 inches (43–86 cm) long. They are smaller than many other kinds of rattlesnakes, and their venom is not as deadly as larger rattlesnakes' venom.

Sidewinders got their name from the way they move. They throw part of their body forward in a loop. Then they move the rest of their body on top of the loop. This helps them move over hot, blowing desert sand. It is called sidewinding because their body moves sideways as they go forward.

Sidewinders are active at night during the hot summer months. They are active during the day in the cooler winter months.

Mojave Rattlesnakes

Mojave rattlesnakes live in the desert and low mountain areas in the southwestern United States and Mexico. They are generally about 22 to 50 inches (56–127 cm) long and are usually brown or green with a dark **diamond** pattern along their back. They are nocturnal, which means they are awake and they hunt at night. They eat mice, rats, and lizards.

Mojave rattlesnakes are one of the deadliest kinds of rattlesnakes in the world. This is because they will strike quickly if they feel they are in danger. Mojave rattlesnake venom can kill people if the bite is left untreated.

Green mojave rattlesnakes, shown here, are sometimes called Mojave greens.

Eastern Diamondbacks

Eastern diamondbacks are another deadly type of rattlesnake. They are brown with dark diamonds outlined in yellow along their back. They live in the southeastern United States and are very large. An eastern diamondback was found in Florida that was 8.8 feet (2.7 m) long. Large eastern diamondbacks can weigh up to 50 pounds (23 kg)!

Eastern diamondbacks are especially deadly because of their size. They can strike a victim that is several feet (m) away from them. They hold enough venom in their big body that if they let all of it out at once, it could kill up to 400 people!

The eastern diamondback rattlesnake is the largest venomous snake in North America. Luckily, this is a shy snake, which does its best to stay away from people.

Rattlesnakes and People

Rattlesnakes can be deadly and people must be careful around them. You should never try to touch a rattlesnake. A hurt rattlesnake can be even more dangerous than a healthy one because it might be quicker to strike. Rattlesnakes will often, but not always, avoid people. The safest place to see rattlesnakes is in a zoo.

Rattlesnakes can help people in several ways. They help control the number of rodents when they prey on them. Some scientists even study their venom. Some rattlesnakes, such as the timber rattlesnake and the ridge-nosed rattlesnake, are **endangered** and people must help protect them.

Glossary

camouflage (KA-muh-flahj) A color or shapes that match what is around something and help hide it.

coil (KOYL) The ring or curl of something that is wound up.

defenses (dih-FEN-sez) Things a living thing does that help keep it safe.

diamond (DY-uh-mund) A shape with four sides.

endangered (in-DAYN-jerd) In danger of no longer existing.

fangs (FANGZ) Sharp teeth that inject venom.

fragile (FRA-jul) Easily broken.

habitat (HA-beh-tat) The places where an animal or a plant naturally lives.

hibernate (HY-bur-nayt) To stay inside during a cold period of time.

predators (PREH-duh-terz) Animals that kill other animals for food.

prey (PRAY) An animal that is hunted by another animal for food.

protein (PROH-teen) An important element inside the cells of plants and animals.

saliva (suh-LY-vuh) The liquid in the mouth that starts to break down food and helps food slide down the throat.

venomous (VEH-nuh-mis) Having a poisonous bite.

Index

C
coil, 12

D
danger, 4, 18
desert, 4, 18

F
face, 4
family, 4

H
habitat, 12

N
noise, 4, 6, 12
North America, 4

P
pits, 4, 10
pit vipers, 4

predators, 4, 10
prey, 4, 8, 10
protein, 6

T
tail, 4, 6

V
Viperidae, 4
vipers, 4

Web Sites

Due to the changing nature of Internet links, PowerKids Press has developed an online list of Web sites related to the subject of this book. This site is updated regularly. Please use this link to access the list:
www.powerkidslinks.com/ssn/rattle/